Published by Led to Lead, Inc.
Printed in the United States of America

MW01601978

Paperback ISBN: 978-0-578-92268-3
Ebook ISBN: 978-0-578-93745-8

Ordering Information:
FX3 Ministries, Inc. books may be purchased in bulk. Special discounts are available on quantity purchases by corporations, associations, and others. Orders by U.S. trade bookstores and wholesalers. For details, contact the publisher at the address listed below. For permission requests, write to the publisher, addressed to:
Attention:
    Permissions
    FX3 Ministries
    13611 S. Dixie Hwy #463
    Miami, FL 33176
    www.faithfirefury.com

Italics in Scripture quotations are the author's emphasis.

Unless otherwise indicated, Scripture quotations are from:
The Holy Bible, English Standard Version (ESV)
© 2001 by Crossway Bibles, a division of Good News Publishers.
Used by permission. All rights reserved.

Other Scripture quotations are from:
The Holy Bible, New International Version (NIV)
© 1973, 1978, 1984, 2011 by Biblica, Inc.™
Used by permission. All rights reserved worldwide.
The Holy Bible, King James Version (KJV)

1st Edition, June 2021

Cover and Interior Design: *Carlos F. Peña*
Cover Photography: *Raw Pixel / © Eberhard Grossgasteiger*

FX3 CHALLENGE

— F A I T H —

A 30-DAY STUDY THROUGH
GOD'S WORD FOR DIRECTION

CARLOS F. PEÑA

LED TO LEAD

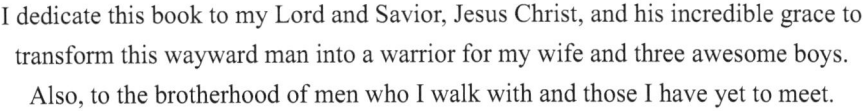

I dedicate this book to my Lord and Savior, Jesus Christ, and his incredible grace to transform this wayward man into a warrior for my wife and three awesome boys. Also, to the brotherhood of men who I walk with and those I have yet to meet.

Most importantly, to my father, who continues to make an impact in my life. I treasure these things daily.

TABLE OF CONTENTS:

Unfortunately, our society constantly tells us that we can have it all with little to no work. Nothing can be further from the truth. Sustainable change and transformation take commitment and effort. For this reason, I created the FX3 Challenge. The FX3 Challenge is a three-phase program developed for men ready to commit and move from complacency to conquering alongside other brothers and the honor of becoming an FX3 Warrior.

HOW TO GET THE MOST OUT OF THE NEXT 30 DAYS.

In life, nothing worthwhile comes easy. Lasting change and transformation takes deliberate effort and time. This reality means that you need both **commitment and consistency** to see results.

These two factors are essential for advancement in any area of your life, especially when embarking on a spiritual growth journey. Miraculous things will happen when you commit to Jesus and the Holy Spirit. God will work in your life to accomplish His will for you. Considering this, the goal for you during these next thirty days is to:

- Discover what Scripture says about being a man.
- Learn how to faithfully and consistently follow Christ and grow spiritually.
- Gain strength, wisdom, and encouragement from a brotherhood.
- Transform your marriage, family, personal and professional relationships.

WHAT TO EXPECT

Before we start, we need to set some initial ground rules and expectations. Adhering to these guidelines will secure the health and growth of yourself and others when taking this journey with a fellow brother or in a group. It will also prevent any potential misunderstandings. But, more importantly, it provides you with focus and direction.

GROUP RULES

RESPECT:

Avoid dismissing others' thoughts, don't laugh at others when they've shared (unless it's a joke), and no put-downs of any kind. Opening up can be hard enough, and this place should be a welcoming place for all to find answers and support. Also, agreeing to disagree on specific points of view. Discussions are about discovery. If a conflict should arise, discuss the issue outside of group time on a one-on-one basis.

CONFIDENTIALITY:

Unfortunately, the saying "What happens in Vegas stays in Vegas" doesn't always prove true. Not the case for this brotherhood. What's said in the group stays in the group. No one wants to find out he has been the subject of gossip or well-meaning "prayer discussions." Violation of this trust is grounds for removal from the group.

LISTEN AND SUPPORT:

We care for one another during the discussions by really listening to what others are sharing. Try to avoid thinking about how you will respond or what you are going to say next. We're not here to "fix" or "rescue" each other. That's Jesus Christ's job through the power of the Holy Spirit. Instead, we listen for the Holy Spirit to provide opportunities to speak into each one of us and let him do the necessary work.

ACCOUNTABILITY:

Similar to listening and support, we approach accountability as the ability to help our brother accomplish his goals as it aligns with God's will. We're not to pass judgment or "shame" someone for falling short. Instead, we help them up, encourage them and remind them of what they are committed to doing.

COMMITMENTS

1   For these next thirty days, I will make **my quiet time with God a priority** by making it the first thing I do in the morning. I will also partner up with a fellow brother and **check in with him regularly.** We will encourage and hold each other accountable. It could be as simple as a text, prayer, call, coffee, etc.

2   I will complete the **Daily Directives and memorize** the weekly memory verse. There are five Daily Directives per week, and *Create Your Own* days. *Create Your Own* days are for me to create my own devotional. Finally, I will complete the three action items for each Daily Directive which are:

Read: Although I may be busy, I will make time for God first, knowing all other things will align. Like food for the body, spiritual food is God's word. Therefore, at the very least, I will read the verse of the day.

Pray: I will also make time to pray as it's essential to my soul. When I pray, I will take a posture of humility and become receptive to hear God's voice and prompting. Consistency is key.

Meditate / Make It Real: I will get the most from my reading and prayer time by journaling my responses to the questions and verses. Journaling makes my thoughts tangible and actionable. I will also track my progress by checking the boxes for each Daily Directive to hold myself accountable and celebrate my accomplishments.

Share: I learn most when I teach what I learned. For this reason, I will take deliberate steps and time to share with others what God is saying to me through my studies.

3   I will come **prepared and ready to share** with my brother or within a group every week. I know the Spirit moves greatest when all of us contribute. I will complete the readings before meeting so that I and others will benefit the most from our time together.

Name: _____ Signature: _____

THE THREE TENETS

Based on 1 Cor. 16:13-14 and expanded upon in the book Faith Fire Fury, an FX3 Warrior lives out his life according to the following three tenets:

Faith: *We believe with complete confidence in God's inerrant Word. We treasure its truths, and respect its reproofs.* We acknowledge the Creator God as our heavenly Father, infinitely perfect and intimately acquainted with all our ways.

We place our hope on the fact that Christ died for our sins, then rose from the dead. Before God, he now declares us to be righteous and new creations. Christ's sacrifice on our behalf demands that we pursue a lifelong process of sanctification through the Spirit.

Fire: *We use our time, talents, gifts, and resources to live every day in a way that glorifies God.* We rely on the Holy Spirit and the Word to empower and continually transform us into the likeness of Christ. To do this, we study His word in depth to apply his teachings to our life.

We believe and accept that our identity and purpose are found in God's word and rely on the Spirit for guidance, empowerment, instruction, and correction.

Fury: *We passionately pursue what God wants us to do. We individually and collectively live sacrificially for others by sharing Christ's love, hope, and message of salvation with the world, and to help others to do the same.*

We're in a spiritual war with forces working against us, trying to prevent us from fulfilling our mission. To be victorious, we individually and collectively fight these battles under God's leadership, according to his word and his example.

MATTHEW 17:20

For truly, I say to you, if you have faith like a grain of mustard seed, you will say to this mountain, 'Move from here to there,' and it will move, and nothing will be impossible for you."

SESSION 1:

WHO IS _____?

Ask any guy at random to describe a man, and he's more than likely to describe a handsome man with a successful career, adventurous, strong, brave, confident, well dressed, and with an adoring woman by his side. The answer is usually a deep-seated desire to be that man. Although many of the attributes mentioned are admirable, most of our perceptions of who we should be are pre-packaged ideals created by someone else and communicated through advertising, TV, movies, and other mass media messages.

Today, "real men" are brave and strong but also sensitive and caring. We're also told to be docile and sentimental but also take charge and steadfast. What?! In essence, we're supposed to know when to be the right man at the right time. Who decides who's right? How can we ever keep up?

Contrast this to when you ask a man to describe themselves, and they may start with their physical characteristics, personality traits, or segway into what they do, what others think, what they have, or what they don't have. But, unfortunately, none of these answers align with who our Creator says we are.

This week you will spend time exploring who you are.

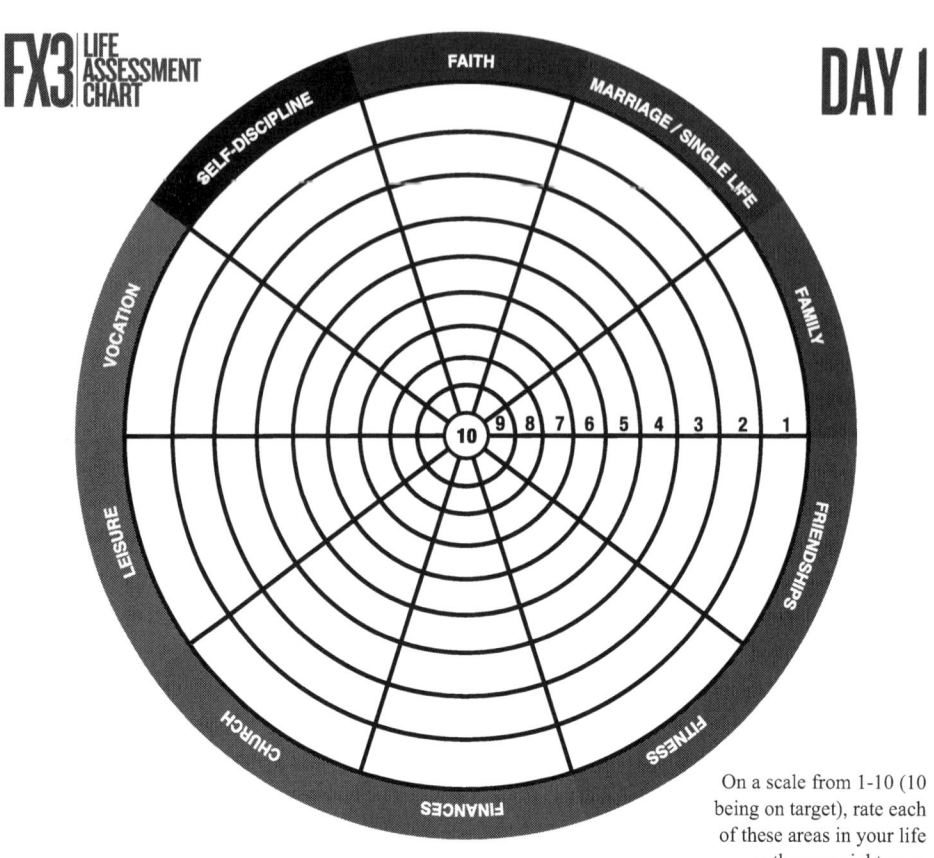

On a scale from 1-10 (10 being on target), rate each of these areas in your life as they are right now.

How do you feel about your life as you look at your chart?

_____

_____

_____

_____

_____

_____

_____

_____

_____

_____

_____

Which of these area(s) would you most like to improve and why?

_____

_____

_____

_____

_____

_____

_____

_____

_____

_____

What would a score of 10 look like in one or all of these areas?

_____

_____

_____

_____

_____

_____

_____

_____

_____

_____

□
WHO IS _____?

Be detailed in describing yourself (physical, spiritual, attitude, behaviors, etc.)

_____

_____

_____

_____

_____

_____

_____

_____

_____

_____

_____

_____

_____

_____

_____

_____

_____

_____

_____

_____

_____

_____

_____

_____

_____

_____

HOW SHOULD OTHERS DESCRIBE YOU?

How would you want your woman, child, friends, colleagues to describe you?

_____

_____

_____

_____

_____

_____

_____

_____

_____

_____

_____

_____

_____

_____

_____

_____

_____

_____

_____

_____

_____

_____

_____

_____

_____

_____

☐
WHAT ARE YOU WILLING TO DO?

What are you willing to do to become the man you want to be?

_____

_____

_____

_____

_____

_____

_____

_____

_____

_____

_____

_____

_____

_____

_____

_____

_____

_____

_____

_____

_____

_____

_____

_____

MANHOOD IS NOT AN AGE. IT'S A MISSION DAY 5

Thirteen years ago today, God blessed us with the arrival of our first son. His life is an example of faith beyond what I ever expected. Before his birth, my wife's doctor told her it would be challenging for her to conceive, if not impossible. Disheartened, she gave me the news.

Without hesitation, I reminded her that God is greater than any man. He can accomplish the impossible for His glory. So, that day, we prayed and dedicated my future child's life to God. Our prayer was that if God were gracious enough to grant us this desire, we would honor him by raising him in his way. We prayed this daily for almost a year.

Then around the year, my wife became pregnant. We rejoiced and made our preparations for his arrival. My wife had a normal pregnancy, and on September 7th, 2007, she delivered a healthy baby boy. Ever since then, every decision regarding his life has involved God. Even his name, "creative gift from God," reflects our dedicating his life to Him.

More than this, I'm witnessing his spiritual and physical transformation to maturity. In this, I, too, continue to be transformed spiritually and physically. When my son was born, the man I was is not the man I am today, nor will I be tomorrow. The reason is that I'm continually being transformed into Christ's likeness and have faith this will never be complete until the day he calls me home.

Many men believe manhood is something you reach at a certain age, a right of passage. However, authentic manhood is not about "arriving" but rather a lifelong pursuit of Godly living through sanctification. Manhood is a continual submission to God's will and transformation, which he will eventually complete when we leave this broken, sin-infected body, and He gives us a new one. Manhood means being on a mission for Christ.

FX3 DAILY DIRECTIVE:

READ:

When I was a child, I spoke like a child, I thought like a child, I reasoned like a child. When I became a man, I gave up childish ways. [12] *For now we see in a mirror dimly, but then face to face. Now I know in part; then I shall know fully, even as I have been fully known.* - **1 Corinthians 13:11-12**

PRAY:

As you prepare to study, pray for the wisdom to understand and apply what you just read. Journal your prayer.

_____

_____

_____

_____

_____

_____

_____

MEDITATE / MAKE IT REAL:

What's your definition of manhood?

_____

_____

_____

_____

_____

_____

_____

_____

MEDITATE / MAKE IT REAL:

According to this passage(s), what am I called to do?

_____

_____

_____

_____

_____

_____

_____

How am I going to apply or do what it says?

_____

_____

_____

_____

_____

_____

SHARE:

Share what you've learned with others.

_____

_____

_____

_____

_____

_____

FX3 DAILY DIRECTIVE:

READ:

PRAY:

As you prepare to study, pray for the wisdom to understand and apply what you just read. Journal your prayer.

_____

_____

_____

_____

_____

_____

_____

MEDITATE / MAKE IT REAL:

How do I see myself in the passage(s) I just read?

_____

_____

_____

_____

_____

_____

_____

MEDITATE / MAKE IT REAL:

☐

According to this passage(s), what am I called to do?

_____

_____

_____

_____

_____

_____

How am I going to apply or do what it says?

_____

_____

_____

_____

_____

_____

SHARE:

Share what you've learned with others.

_____

_____

_____

_____

_____

_____

FX3 DAILY DIRECTIVE: _____

READ:

PRAY:

As you prepare to study, pray for the wisdom to understand and apply what you just read. Journal your prayer.

_____

_____

_____

_____

_____

_____

_____

MEDITATE / MAKE IT REAL:

How do I see myself in the passage(s) I just read?

_____

_____

_____

_____

_____

_____

_____

MEDITATE / MAKE IT REAL:

According to this passage(s), what am I called to do?

_____

_____

_____

_____

_____

How am I going to apply or do what it says?

_____

_____

_____

_____

_____

SHARE:

Share what you've learned with others.

_____

_____

_____

_____

_____

SESSION 2:

THE WORLD NEEDS THE TRUE YOU

MEMORY VERSE OF THE WEEK

I PETER 2:9

But you are a chosen people, a royal priesthood, a holy nation, God's special possession, that you may declare the praises of him who called you out of darkness into his wonderful light.

A few years ago, we moved into a nice neighborhood with well-kept homes, friendly neighbors, and children playing on the streets. Working from my desk one evening, I heard the faint sound of screaming outside. "On my G-d, Oh my G-d!" Concerned, I got up and went to the front of the house to see what was going on. As soon as I peered through the front window, I saw my neighbor walking down the street, dragging a carry-on behind him. He was casually walking down the middle of the road. Ignoring the screams of his wife, marching on until he was out of sight. After speaking with him, it seems he'd "had enough" of his wife and just wanted to "get out."

Compare this to another man I knew who dedicated decades to his career and company. He worked for a travel company for over twenty-five years, spending almost 300 days out of the year traveling the world. During his time with the company, he earned multiple industry accolades and recognitions. Then, one day, they decided to terminate his position. They gave him severance pay of a few months and wished him the best. But, once "grounded," as they say in the industry, he came home to an empty house. After being neglected for so many years, his wife filed for divorce. During that same time, his children moved away for college. He then found himself alone, without a wife, family, or career.

Unfortunately, there are many other stories just like this with the same results. It saddens my soul to see men and those around them suffer needlessly. The collateral damage caused by chasing lies and false expectations are catastrophic. The problem is most of the damage is not always immediately visible. It's like the person that suntanned too much in their youth is diagnosed with skin cancer later in life. The damage which is apparent today started long ago. Another issue is that many live unfulfilled lives. They live a cycle of routines rather than a riveting and fulfilling life for themselves and those around them. These consequences result from men not knowing who God says they are and seeking their purpose and validation outside God's word. This journey will help you dispel fact from fiction and replace lies with truth about what it means to be a man.

THE WORLD NEEDS THE TRUE YOU
YOUR WOMAN NEEDS THE TRUE YOU

Today there are countless incidences where women are starting to call men out publicly for abusing their position and authority to take advantage of women—both personally and professionally. There is a crazy amount of discourse and arguments relating to women's and men's rights in today's world. The world has decided to prioritize one over the other. There are extremes. For decades there's been a battle of who will emerge victoriously. Who's right?

The problem with this perspective, they're both incorrect. One is not better than the other. One should not be more important than the other. Instead, we need to focus on the strengths and weaknesses of each. We need to recognize and embrace that men and women are different. God created us differently in His providence and wisdom to complement each other, not dominate each other. A recent study revealed women aren't looking for men who invest all their energy in trying to prove how strong, manly, masculine, macho, or heroic they are. They want a man who is willing to meet them where they are and treat them fairly and equitably—this also includes the desire to keep the romantic sparks burning. Notice the order of priorities. Women want first to be understood, then cared for, and finally intimate. Men's default is usually the other way around. We want intimacy first, then provision, and finally, care and love.

Contrast this to a man's deepest desire, respect, and it's no wonder there's confusion on meeting expectations between men and women. According to *Love & Respect* author Dr. Emerson Eggerichs, "When a husband feels disrespected, he has a natural tendency to react in ways that feel unloving to his wife. Likewise, when a wife feels unloved, she has a natural tendency to react in ways that feel disrespectful to her husband." In essence, a man expresses the love and affection his partner seeks when he feels respected. But the real question is whether the man supposed to love first or the woman show respect first?

FX3 DAILY DIRECTIVE:

READ:

Likewise, husbands, live with your wives in an understanding way, showing honor to the woman as the weaker vessel, since they are heirs with you of the grace of life, so that your prayers may not be hindered.

1 Peter 3:7

PRAY:

As you prepare to study, pray for the wisdom to understand and apply what you just read. Journal your prayer.

_____

_____

_____

_____

_____

_____

_____

MEDITATE / MAKE IT REAL:

How are you currently treating the woman in your life?

_____

_____

_____

_____

_____

_____

_____

MEDITATE / MAKE IT REAL:

According to this passage(s), what am I called to do?

_____

_____

_____

_____

_____

_____

_____

How am I going to apply or do what it says?

_____

_____

_____

_____

_____

_____

_____

SHARE:

Share what you've learned with others.

_____

_____

_____

_____

_____

_____

_____

THE WORLD NEEDS THE TRUE YOU
YOUR CHILDREN NEED THE TRUE YOU

A few years ago, there was a movie that spoke volumes to me. It was *The Tree of Life*, written and directed by Terrence Malick. This unconventional film challenged moviegoers and me to stretch our minds and souls as we follow a Texan family in the 1950's family through their lives. Jack O'Brien (Hunter McCracken) is the joy of his mother (Jessica Chastain) and his father (Brad Pitt). Through a succession of varying scenes, we see him growing up and developing as a person. The movie focuses on Jack's perspective and his relationships with his father, mother, and brother. The story's central theme is how Jack tries to process and struggles to understand the dynamics between his father's controlling nature and his mother's nurturing qualities. However, what impacted me the most was Jack's relationship with his father.

Throughout the movie, we get glimpses of Jack's rigid and domineering father constantly criticizing Jack. There are scenes where he loses his temper, belittles Jack, and is often distant and removed from him. Later, we catch a glimpse of how this impacts Jack when there is a time he vows to kill his father, but when he has a chance while his father is underneath the car, he doesn't act. Despite all this, there is a moment when Jack, as a boy, realizes he is more like his father than his mother. This realization saddens him because of the great value he places on his mother's seemingly opposite qualities. Yet Jack also recalls instances of witnessing his father's vulnerabilities and glimpses of showing love.

This movie reminds me how much influence a father or father figure can have on a child's life. Unfortunately, today, many men have been negatively impacted by growing up without a solid and healthy father figure. Many of us grew up with fathers who showed love to us through hard work, discipline, toughness, or any other way but emotionally. For others, fathers were not even in the picture. Yet others can attest to having great relationships with their fathers. Regardless, we must recognize the influential and life-long impact a man can have on his children or those under his care.

FX3 DAILY DIRECTIVE:

READ:

These commandments that I give you today are to be on your hearts. Impress them on your children. Talk about them when you sit at home and when you walk along the road, when you lie down and when you get up. - **Deuteronomy 6:6-7**

PRAY:

As you prepare to study, pray for the wisdom to understand and apply what you just read. Journal your prayer.

_____

_____

_____

_____

_____

_____

_____

MEDITATE / MAKE IT REAL:

How are you currently leading your child or children under your care or influence?

_____

_____

_____

_____

_____

_____

_____

MEDITATE / MAKE IT REAL:

According to this passage(s), what am I called to do?

_____

_____

_____

_____

_____

_____

How am I going to apply or do what it says?

_____

_____

_____

_____

_____

_____

SHARE:

Share what you've learned with others.

_____

_____

_____

_____

_____

_____

THE WORLD NEEDS THE TRUE YOU
YOUR FRIENDS NEED THE TRUE YOU

I still remember my very first best friend, Rodrigo. We were in pre-kindergarten and immediately took to each other. The years that followed included jumping off balconies, running wild on bikes, teasing girls, playing video games, and all sorts of mayhem. Eventually, life intervened, and our families moved apart. In time, I lost contact with Rodrigo. After that, my family moved around some more.

Over the years, I've experienced similar outcomes and eventually coped with this disappointment by not investing too much into making close friendships. As a result, I did have many acquaintances but very little to no true friends. However, that slowly changed over time, and not long ago, I received confirmation on the importance of friendship even when I didn't realize it.

"What's up, brother?" Rodrigo asked as we spoke for the first time in almost thirty years. It was so great hearing his voice. He told me how for quite some time, he wanted to reconnect to say something important. But, for some reason or another, he never got around to reaching out. Finally, after much insistence, his wife convinced him to contact me. He told me he wanted to thank my family and me for our impression on his life so long ago and how leading him to Jesus changed his life. He went on to tell me about his faith and encouraged me to continue doing what I'm doing. His call came at an opportune time as I felt defeated, questioning my investment in relationships. Renewed and confirmed, I thanked God for his call as an answered prayer.

What I learned that day was the importance of developing friendships, especially close ones, and the lasting impact it can have on a person when it is Kingdom-focused. Friendship is a contradiction in that the more you give, the more you receive. True friendship is for the benefit of others and requires real men to make themselves vulnerable. Friendships have the power to create lasting impressions. Some good, others bad. The most treasured friendships are those in which we're raw and open with each other. True friendships are about shouldering the pains and sharing the victories of life.

FX3 DAILY DIRECTIVE:

READ:

Two are better than one, because they have a good reward for their toil. ¹⁰ For if they fall, one will lift up his fellow. But woe to him who is alone when he falls and has not another to lift him up! ¹¹ Again, if two lie together, they keep warm, but how can one keep warm alone? ¹² And though a man might prevail against one who is alone, two will withstand him—a threefold cord is not quickly broken. - **Ecclesiastes 4:9-12**

PRAY:

As you prepare to study, pray for the wisdom to understand and apply what you just read. Journal your prayer.

_____

_____

_____

_____

_____

_____

_____

MEDITATE / MAKE IT REAL:

What are you doing to form or strengthen friendships? If not, what's stopping you?

_____

_____

_____

_____

_____

_____

_____

MEDITATE / MAKE IT REAL:

According to this passage(s), what am I called to do?

_____

_____

_____

_____

_____

_____

How am I going to apply or do what it says?

_____

_____

_____

_____

_____

_____

SHARE:

Share what you've learned with others.

_____

_____

_____

_____

_____

_____

THE WORLD NEEDS THE TRUE YOU
YOUR COLLEAGUES NEED THE TRUE YOU

In 2006, Siemens, one of Germany's biggest companies, was exposed to one of the world's most notable and massive corruption scandals. Courts convicted Siemens of paying bribes to government officials and civil servants worldwide, amounting to approximately US$1.4 billion. Before the corruption scandal, Siemens had a highly reputable and professional company image. They were known worldwide for their technological products and reliable services in telecommunications, power, transportation, and medical equipment. They portrayed a squeaky-clean corporate age from the outside, but they were anything but honest behind the scenes. Investigators discovered how Siemens went on a ten-year global corruption strategy to pay off officials and decision-makers as a way to gain market share and increase its price. It seems they found loopholes in a few countries' legal systems, including Germany, and used it to their advantage.

As the investigation unfolded, they also discovered the corruption came from the top down. One Siemens employee, Siekaczek, said, "We all knew that what we were doing was illegal. Paying a bribe was customary in practically all business units at Siemens AG, except for business units that deals with lamps and such." In the end, Siemens paid more than $1.6 billion in fines, penalties, and disgorgement of profits, including $800 million to US authorities. Along with the penalties, mass staff changes also came about. The first was ousting CEO Klaus Kleinfeld and replacing him with Peter Löscher. When Peter took over, he replaced about 80% of the top-level executives, 70% of the next level down, and 40% below that level. Going further, they also changed how the managing board made decisions and worked to streamline their global operating units.

Sadly, stories like this are becoming the norm in company culture. Leaders with integrity and principles are not always recognized or valued in a world that regards fame and power as the pinnacle of success. As a Christian, living according to God's word is fundamental for living a righteous life as it will provide the example your colleagues need the most.

FX3 DAILY DIRECTIVE:

READ:

So if there is any encouragement in Christ, any comfort from love, any participation in the Spirit, any affection and sympathy, complete my joy by being of the same mind, having the same love, being in full accord and of one mind. Do nothing from rivalry or conceit, but in humility count others more significant than yourselves. Let each of you look not only to his own interests, but also to the interests of others. - **Philippians 2:1-3**

PRAY:

As you prepare to study, pray for the wisdom to understand and apply what you just read. Journal your prayer.

_____

_____

_____

_____

_____

_____

_____

MEDITATE / MAKE IT REAL:

How are you, or can you look out for the interests of others?

_____

_____

_____

_____

_____

_____

_____

_____

MEDITATE / MAKE IT REAL:

According to this passage(s), what am I called to do?

_____

_____

_____

_____

_____

_____

How am I going to apply or do what it says?

_____

_____

_____

_____

_____

_____

SHARE:

Share what you've learned with others.

_____

_____

_____

_____

_____

_____

THE WORLD NEEDS THE TRUE YOU

DAY 12

There's an inspirational story out there of a small village on a rocky seacoast, where storms often battered, and seas were ever treacherous. Unfortunately, many ships crashed onto the rocks by the storms. As a result, many sailors lost their lives due to the raging seas. Troubled by the situation, the people decided to establish a lighthouse and life-saving station to warn ships away from the rocks and save the lives of those cast into the icy waters. After gathering the funds and securing the necessary materials and equipment, they built a tower and set a beacon. They also made a lookout system and purchased boats to help with rescuing sailors out at sea. They were now in the business of saving lives!

As a result of their efforts, fewer ships went on the rocks. Also, when such a tragedy did occur, the people risked their own lives to rescue those cast into the raging, icy waters. Within a few short years, people came from all over to study their lighthouse and use it as a model. In time, the lighthouse became more than just a warning system; it also became a place for people to gather and fellowship. The lighthouse soon became the center of life in the little town. Over the years, the lighthouse served as a life-saving structure by warning ships and picking up sailors from the bitter cold icy waters. It represented safety, comfort, and a life-saving beacon of hope for those sailing in the darkness.

This story is an example of how many lost people in this world travel in darkness and don't realize they need a saving light. Unfortunately, this world is fraught with dangers lying in wait to destroy, capsize, and smash people sailing through life. For this reason, God calls you to be the beacon of light this world so desperately needs. So, even though we have a mission of reaching the lost beyond our borders, we can start where we are today.

FX3 DAILY DIRECTIVE:

READ:

"You are the light of the world. A city set on a hill cannot be hidden. [15] Nor do people light a lamp and put it under a basket, but on a stand, and it gives light to all in the house. [16] In the same way, let your light shine before others, so that they may see your good works and give glory to your Father who is in heaven." - **Matthew 5:14-16**

PRAY:

As you prepare to study, pray for the wisdom to understand and apply what you just read. Journal your prayer.

_____

_____

_____

_____

_____

_____

MEDITATE / MAKE IT REAL:

How are you, or can you be a light unto the world?

_____

_____

_____

_____

_____

_____

_____

MEDITATE / MAKE IT REAL:

□

According to this passage(s), what am I called to do?

_____

_____

_____

_____

_____

_____

_____

How am I going to apply or do what it says?

_____

_____

_____

_____

_____

_____

_____

SHARE:

Share what you've learned with others.

_____

_____

_____

_____

_____

_____

_____

FX3 DAILY DIRECTIVE:

READ:

DAY 13

PRAY:

As you prepare to study, pray for the wisdom to understand and apply what you just read. Journal your prayer.

_____

_____

_____

_____

_____

_____

_____

MEDITATE / MAKE IT REAL:

How do I see myself in the passage(s) I just read?

_____

_____

_____

_____

_____

_____

_____

_____

MEDITATE / MAKE IT REAL: ☐

According to this passage(s), what am I called to do?

_____

_____

_____

_____

_____

_____

_____

How am I going to apply or do what it says?

_____

_____

_____

_____

_____

_____

SHARE:

Share what you've learned with others.

_____

_____

_____

_____

_____

_____

FX3 DAILY DIRECTIVE: _____

DAY 14

READ:

PRAY:

As you prepare to study, pray for the wisdom to understand and apply what you just read. Journal your prayer.

_____

_____

_____

_____

_____

_____

_____

MEDITATE / MAKE IT REAL:

How do I see myself in the passage(s) I just read?

_____

_____

_____

_____

_____

_____

_____

MEDITATE / MAKE IT REAL: ☐

According to this passage(s), what am I called to do?

_____

_____

_____

_____

_____

_____

_____

How am I going to apply or do what it says?

_____

_____

_____

_____

_____

_____

SHARE:

Share what you've learned with others.

_____

_____

_____

_____

_____

_____

SESSION 3:

THE COUNTERFEITS

MEMORY VERSE OF THE WEEK

JOHN 8:44

He was a murderer from the beginning, and does not stand in the truth, because there is no truth in him. When he lies, he speaks out of his own character, for he is a liar and the father of lies.

In the late 1970s and early 1980s, Barry Bremen became known as the Great Impostor for his outrageous stunts. He once posed as a baseball umpire at the World Series, a player in an MLB All-Star Game, a player in an NBA All-Star Game, a referee in the NFL, a Dallas Cowboys cheerleader, and a professional golfer.

He lived by the motto "No guts, no glory." Ironically, he dissuaded copycats by telling them, "Don't do it. It's against the law. Stay away. This is my act."

He was so audacious in his impostor stunts that he once attempted to pose for a group picture with future Hall of Famers George Brett, Reggie Jackson, Joe Morgan, Mike Schmidt, Gaylord Perry, Dave Winfield, Steve Carlton, Nolan Ryan, Carl Yastrzemski, Lou Brock, and Tommy Lasorda. During one of his last stunts, Bremen got up and accepted a Best Supporting Actress award for Hill Street Blues actress Betty Thomas at the 1985 Emmy Awards. He was arrested and later apologized to Thomas, telling her he thought she wasn't there to accept the award.

Barry's story is similar to that of many men as they walk around posing as something they're not. By being or using counterfeits, they're attempting mask or medicate a deeper issue or illness—the loss of identity and significance. This illness manifests itself in unresolved questions: Am I a man? And what's my purpose in life? When these questions go unanswered, we set off to find a solution—in anything or anyone that seems to offer an answer.

The problem with trying to cure this illness on our own is that we can't. We'll spend our lives seeking the cure, many times treating symptoms rather than the illness itself. But only God provides the real treatment. Anything else is an impostor, a poser, a lie, a counterfeit.

THE COUNTERFEITS
WHAT IS A REAL MAN?

The answer to this million-dollar question eludes most men. Ask any guy at random to describe manhood, and he's more than likely to describe a handsome man with a successful career, a man who's adventurous, strong, brave, confident, and well-dressed, and with an adoring woman by his side. Although many of these attributes are admirable, most of our perceptions of manhood come from advertising, TV, movies, and other mass media messages—which are continuously redefining manhood.

Nothing describes the current confusion better than a New York Times article by Jessica Bennett about Dr. Michael Kimmel. Dr. Kimmel is an expert on men and masculinity, and served as a professor of sociology and gender studies at Stony Brook University in New York. Ms. Bennett was writing a story on Dr. Kimmel, and her research led her to sit in on one of his classes. She writes:

> Michael Kimmel stood in front of a classroom in blue jeans, and, a blazer with a pen to a whiteboard, asked, "What does it mean to be a good man?" The students looked puzzled.
>
> "Let's say it was said at your funeral, 'He was a good man,'" Dr. Kimmel explained. "What does that mean to you?"
>
> "Caring," a male student in the front said. "Putting other's needs before yours," another young man said. "Honest," a third said. Dr. Kimmel listed each term under the heading "Good Man," then turned back to the group. "Now," he said, "tell me what it means to be a real man." This time, the students reacted more quickly. "Take charge; be authoritative," said James, a sophomore. "Take risks," said Amanda, a sociology graduate student. "It means suppressing any kind of weakness," another offered. "I think for me being a real man meant talk like a man," said a young man who'd grown up in Turkey. "Walk like a man. Never cry."
>
> Dr. Kimmel had been taking notes. "Now you're in the wheelhouse," he said, excitedly. He pointed to the "Good Man" list on the left side of the board, then to the "Real Man" list he'd added to the right. "Look at the disparity. I think American men are confused about what it means to be a man."

FX3 DAILY DIRECTIVE:

READ:

Be watchful, stand firm in the faith, act like men, be strong. [14] Let all that you do be done in love. - **1 Corinthians 16:13-14**

PRAY:

As you prepare to study, pray for the wisdom to understand and apply what you just read. Journal your prayer.

_____

_____

_____

_____

_____

_____

_____

MEDITATE / MAKE IT REAL:

How would you define a "real" man?

_____

_____

_____

_____

_____

_____

_____

MEDITATE / MAKE IT REAL:

According to this passage(s), what am I called to do?

_____

_____

_____

_____

_____

_____

How am I going to apply or do what it says?

_____

_____

_____

_____

_____

_____

SHARE:

Share what you've learned with others.

_____

_____

_____

_____

_____

_____

THE COUNTERFEITS
POWER

A polarizing figure in business and life in the nineteenth and early twentieth centuries, John D. Rockefeller was an American industrialist and philanthropist, and the country's first billionaire. At the height of his business empire, his Standard Oil Company refined as much as 90 percent of America's oil. This market dominance made him the wealthiest man of his time, and arguably in history. Although his accomplishments are famous, few people today are aware of how greatly his father impacted his life.

John was the eldest son (and second of six children) of a traveling physician and snake-oil salesman named William ("Big Bill") Avery Rockefeller. For the first years of his life, the family lived in upstate New York, with William making a living through various shady business ventures—from pretending to be a deaf and blind peddler to posing as a doctor to hawk patent medicines. At sixteen John dropped out of high school and worked as an assistant bookkeeper with Hewitt & Tuttle. Shortly after, John decided to start his own business with a partner as a commission merchant in hay, meats, grains, and other goods.

In time, John formed the Standard Oil Company, which became the very first American monopoly. At its height, critics accused Rockefeller and his company of unfair labor and business practices. As a result, the government stepped in and passed laws that led to Standard Oil's breakup. Later, investigative journalist named Ida Tarbell published various articles portraying John as being obsessed with money, a man who was intimidating, secretive, and driven only by ambition. Tarbell also accused Rockefeller's father of posing as a physician and taking advantage of others for financial gain.

The image of power and success that John D. Rockefeller had spent years crafting began to tarnish. He was both incensed and humiliated by the exposé of his unstable father. He spent the rest of his life trying to counteract the negative publicity through ambitious philanthropic endeavors.

FX3 DAILY DIRECTIVE:

READ:

Abide in me, and I in you. As the branch cannot bear fruit by itself, unless it abides in the vine, neither can you, unless you abide in me. [5] I am the vine; you are the branches. Whoever abides in me and I in him, he it is that bears much fruit, for apart from me you can do nothing. - **John 15:4-5**

PRAY:

As you prepare to study, pray for the wisdom to understand and apply what you just read. Journal your prayer.

_____

_____

_____

_____

_____

_____

MEDITATE / MAKE IT REAL:

What is your definition and perspective on power?

_____

_____

_____

_____

_____

_____

MEDITATE / MAKE IT REAL:

□

According to this passage(s), what am I called to do?

_____

_____

_____

_____

_____

_____

How am I going to apply or do what it says?

_____

_____

_____

_____

_____

SHARE:

Share what you've learned with others.

_____

_____

_____

_____

_____

_____

THE COUNTERFEITS
PLEASURE

Growing up, I remember being entranced by James Bond movies. James Bond was a character created by British author, journalist, and naval intelligence officer Ian Fleming. Fleming came up with the fictional character in 1952 when he started writing his first book, *Casino Royale*, at his Goldeneye estate in Jamaica. Ironically, he got the name for his character from American ornithologist James Bond, a Caribbean bird expert and author. He later explained why he chose to use this name: "It struck me that this brief, unromantic, Anglo-Saxon and yet very masculine name was just what I needed."

What appealed to many men (and me) about James Bond was his lifestyle of flying on private planes, driving exotic cars, having beautiful women on his arm, wearing stylish suits, and living lavishly. James had it all. In every Bond film, he seems to indulge in every form of pleasure possible to man. Ironically, Fleming's original idea for the fictional Bond character didn't include excessive drinking, womanizing, and an extravagant lifestyle. If you go back to the author's original writings, Bond's world was less exotic. However, moviemakers didn't like this persona and decided to redefine the fictional character to appeal more to men's deep desires.

Many of the actors playing 007 got tired of playing the part. For example, Daniel Craig was once asked if he would take on another Bond movie. His response: "I'd rather break this glass and slash my wrists. No, not at the moment. Not at all. That's fine. I'm over it at the moment. We're done. All I want to do is move on." He then went on to say, "If I did another Bond movie, it would only be for the money." Sure enough, he later agreed to play 007 one last time—in *No Time to Die*, for an estimated USD \$25 million.

Like the fictional James Bond, many men seek their identity in the stereotyped pleasures of this world. This false belief manifests itself in many forms, such as women, drugs, entertainment, sports, and games. Ultimately, chasing these things for fulfillment and significance leads to emptiness. Trying to fill the void with worldly pleasure leads only to an insatiable hunger for more.

FX3 DAILY DIRECTIVE:

READ:

Since therefore Christ suffered in the flesh, arm yourselves with the same way of thinking, for whoever has suffered in the flesh has ceased from sin, [2] *so as to live for the rest of the time in the flesh no longer for human passions but for the will of God.*
1 Peter 4:1-2

PRAY:

As you prepare to study, pray for the wisdom to understand and apply what you just read. Journal your prayer.

_____

_____

_____

_____

_____

_____

_____

MEDITATE / MAKE IT REAL:

What is your definition and perspective on pleasure?

_____

_____

_____

_____

_____

_____

_____

MEDITATE / MAKE IT REAL:

According to this passage(s), what am I called to do?

_____

_____

_____

_____

_____

_____

How am I going to apply or do what it says?

_____

_____

_____

_____

_____

_____

SHARE:

Share what you've learned with others.

_____

_____

_____

_____

_____

_____

THE COUNTERFEITS
POSSESSIONS

Melvin A. Fisher was a famous Florida treasure hunter in the twentieth century, and a somewhat controversial public figure. Mel claimed that he initially caught the treasure-hunting as a child. However, Mel put this dream on hold when he set off to study engineering at Purdue University after graduating from high school. Shortly after leaving Purdue, he felt a calling to join the World War II effort and enlisted in the service, where he trained with the U.S. Army Corps of Engineers. After completing his service, he returned home, got married and decided to open California's first dive shop on his family's chicken ranch in Torrance.

Fisher managed to find nominal success by offering dive lessons and selling equipment, including snorkel gear that he modified. His love for diving kept increasing, so that in 1953, he sold the chicken ranch to dedicate himself full-time to the dive business. The treasure fever eventually deepened its hold on the Fishers, and in 1962 they abandoned the diving business and moved to Florida's East Coat to search for sunken treasure.

After spending over twenty years searching for a famous ship called the *Nuestra Senora de Atocha*, they eventually discovered her sister ship, the *Santa Margarita* (worth twenty million dollars), but the *Atocha* herself still eluded them. Finally, in 1985, they found it—with a cargo estimated at nearly half a billion dollars. Unfortunately, even this amount of treasure wasn't enough for Mel; in 1998, he admitted selling several counterfeit gold coins at his gift shop in Key West. As a result, he agreed to repay purchasers the prices of the coins— between $2,500 to $10,000 each. In the end, more than $67,000 was paid out to identified claimants.

Mel's story reminds us how the counterfeit of basing our life on possessions is futile and fleeting. Despite having collected almost half a billion dollars in salvage treasure, this still wasn't enough. It seems possessions (or repossessions) will never be enough. There will always be "one more" treasure out there.

FX3 DAILY DIRECTIVE:

READ:

"Do not lay up for yourselves treasures on earth, where moth and rust[a] destroy and where thieves break in and steal, [20] *but lay up for yourselves treasures in heaven, where neither moth nor rust destroys and where thieves do not break in and steal.* [21] *For where your treasure is, there your heart will be also.* - **Matthew 6:19-21**

PRAY:

As you prepare to study, pray for the wisdom to understand and apply what you just read. Journal your prayer.

_____

_____

_____

_____

_____

_____

MEDITATE / MAKE IT REAL:

What is your definition and perspective on possessions?

_____

_____

_____

_____

_____

_____

_____

MEDITATE / MAKE IT REAL:

□

According to this passage(s), what am I called to do?

_____

_____

_____

_____

_____

_____

_____

How am I going to apply or do what it says?

_____

_____

_____

_____

_____

_____

_____

SHARE:

Share what you've learned with others.

_____

_____

_____

_____

_____

_____

_____

THE COUNTERFEITS
PRAISE

Growing up, I remember my father being a stern and very demanding disciplinarian, and his way of showing love was by providing for us. He always worked hard to ensure that we never went without, and that we had more opportunities than he had known. This unselfish desire was for us to have a better life without our having to experience the same heartaches and disappointments he had faced. As a result, he was constantly pushing us to be successful. He didn't want us to endure the struggles he had as an immigrant. He reasoned that if he paid the price for us, we would reap the benefits later.

My father defined success as having a professional career, money in the bank, a good education, a home in a nice neighborhood, and a good reputation. Although these are all admirable goals, I erroneously assumed that his acceptance of me, and my significance as a man, was dependent on my achievement of these goals. I set out to prove to him and everyone else that I could do it—I could be successful. I would study harder, hustle, and eventually make a name for myself. I was going to do this on my own!

I chased after awards, status, prestige, and money. As a result, I became a prideful and angry person. I was also slow to admit mistakes, and I rarely apologized. However, one day, God took his providential hand and got my attention in a way that was like a slap upside the head. As I looked closer at my accomplishments in life, I realized that all my achievements were masking the deep hurt of a painful thought: *What if I'm not enough?* I sought affirmation and significance in and through everything except God.

Many men grow up believing they're loved only when they get praised. Human beings have a deep desire to be recognized, affirmed, and accepted. However, when we recognize that everything we have and can accomplish comes from God, we eradicate sinful pride. Then we can praise God and take joy in a job well done, giving all glory to God.

FX3 DAILY DIRECTIVE:

READ:

Enter his gates with thanksgiving, and his courts with praise! Give thanks to him; bless his name! [5] *For the Lord is good; his steadfast love endures forever, and his faithfulness to all generations.* - **Psalm 100:4–5**

PRAY:

As you prepare to study, pray for the wisdom to understand and apply what you just read. Journal your prayer.

_____

_____

_____

_____

_____

_____

MEDITATE / MAKE IT REAL:

What is your definition and perspective on praise?

_____

_____

_____

_____

_____

_____

_____

MEDITATE / MAKE IT REAL:

☐

According to this passage(s), what am I called to do?

_____

_____

_____

_____

_____

_____

How am I going to apply or do what it says?

_____

_____

_____

_____

_____

_____

SHARE:

Share what you've learned with others.

_____

_____

_____

_____

_____

_____

As the "unsinkable" *Titanic* set out from Southampton, England on her maiden voyage across the Atlantic more than a century ago, the vessel was touted as "the safest ship ever built." But the tragedy that so quickly brought down the *Titanic* resulted in the drowning of more than 1,500 passengers and crew in the icy waters of the north Atlantic. This shocking loss brought about thorough investigations by the United States and Britain, resulting in many new safety protocols and maritime regulations that are still followed today.

These investigations revealed various avoidable situations and human decisions that contributed to the tragedy. On the fourth night of the voyage—the evening of April 14, 1912—the *Titanic* had received a number of warnings from other ships about drifting ice in the area. However, those warnings weren't treated with any urgency, and the ship proceeded at full steam ahead. About twenty minutes before midnight, when lookouts sighted an iceberg in the immediate path of the speeding *Titanic*, there wasn't time enough to turn the ship. She struck the iceberg, resulting in a 300-foot gash that ruptured at least five of its supposedly watertight compartments. Various survivors described the evacuation process as haphazard and uncoordinated. Over the next few hours, passengers witnessed both cowardly and courageous acts. In the end, only 706 out of 2,200 passengers and crew survived.

Besides the speed of the ship and her failure to adequately address the warnings about drifting ice, the investigations also cited a lack of proper crew training and preparation, as well as the overall passive and overconfident attitude of those responsible. The investigators also charged the captain and the crew of the *Californian* (a ship about twenty nautical miles from the Titanic) with failure to respond to the *Titanic's* distress signals. Their report also cited a "laxity of regulation and hasty inspection." British investigators added that the *Californian* "might have saved many, if not all, of the lives that were lost."

FX3 DAILY DIRECTIVE:

READ:

So whoever knows the right thing to do and fails to do it, for him it is sin.

James 4:17

PRAY:

As you prepare to study, pray for the wisdom to understand and apply what you just read. Journal your prayer.

_____

_____

_____

_____

_____

_____

_____

MEDITATE / MAKE IT REAL:

What is your definition and perspective on passivity?

_____

_____

_____

_____

_____

_____

_____

MEDITATE / MAKE IT REAL:

According to this passage(s), what am I called to do?

_____

_____

_____

_____

_____

_____

How am I going to apply or do what it says?

_____

_____

_____

_____

_____

_____

SHARE:

Share what you've learned with others.

_____

_____

_____

_____

_____

_____

FX3 DAILY DIRECTIVE: _____

READ:

PRAY:

As you prepare to study, pray for the wisdom to understand and apply what you just read. Journal your prayer.

_____

_____

_____

_____

_____

_____

_____

MEDITATE / MAKE IT REAL:

How do I see myself in the passage(s) I just read?

_____

_____

_____

_____

_____

_____

_____

_____

MEDITATE / MAKE IT REAL: □

According to this passage(s), what am I called to do?

_____

_____

_____

_____

_____

_____

How am I going to apply or do what it says?

_____

_____

_____

_____

_____

_____

SHARE:

Share what you've learned with others.

_____

_____

_____

_____

_____

_____

FX3 DAILY DIRECTIVE:

READ:

PRAY:

As you prepare to study, pray for the wisdom to understand and apply what you just read. Journal your prayer.

_____

_____

_____

_____

_____

_____

_____

MEDITATE / MAKE IT REAL:

How do I see myself in the passage(s) I just read?

_____

_____

_____

_____

_____

_____

_____

_____

MEDITATE / MAKE IT REAL:

According to this passage(s), what am I called to do?

_____

_____

_____

_____

_____

_____

How am I going to apply or do what it says?

_____

_____

_____

_____

_____

_____

SHARE:

Share what you've learned with others.

_____

_____

_____

_____

_____

_____

SESSION 4:

THE SOURCE

MEMORY VERSE OF THE WEEK

ROMANS 5:12

"Therefore, just as sin came into the world through one man, and death through sin, and so death spread to all men because all sinned -"

In the late 1930's Dr. Willem Kolff, while working in a small ward at the University of Groningen Hospital in the Netherlands, watched helplessly as a young man died slowly of kidney failure. Moved by the event, he decided he would find a way to create a machine that would do the kidneys' work. Unfortunately, the timing was not the best, as shortly after Kolff began his research, World War II broke out. The war and subsequent occupation of the Netherlands by the Germans resulted in Kolff being shipped off to work in a remote Dutch hospital.

Undeterred by his commitment to finding a solution, Kolff improvised, using sausage skins, orange juice cans, a washing machine, and other everyday items to make a device that could clear the blood of toxins. After years of toiling with his invention, Kolff introduced a working prototype in 1943. Although the device was less than optimal, he conducted treatments on patients but unfortunately, he had little success. His big breakthrough came in 1945 when a 67-year-old woman in a uremic coma regained consciousness after 11 hours of hemodialysis with Kolff's dialyzer. Although only one treatment turned out successful, he continued to experiment in improving his design.

After the war, he came to the U.S. and continued his research at Mount Sinai hospital, intending to establish a kidney treatment service. But, once again, he encountered obstacles when hospital administrators opposed the idea, resulting in Kolff and his colleagues conducting treatments in a surgical suite after hours. Then, after a few more years of experimentation and improvements, Kolff and his team finally had a successfully running dialyzer.

Once considered "unsustainable" by many professionals, Dialysis is today performed on nearly 500,000 patients in the U.S. This fantastic invention reminds me of how we all suffer from an incurable disease that requires us to be purified. The disease of sin ravages us, and only Christ can cleanse us. As we await a new body and eternal home, we too must continually be purified by Christ.

THE SOURCE
IN THE BEGINNING

To understand the disease and illnesses of sin that plague humanity and its ramifications on everyday life, we need to go to the source. Genesis 1:1 starts with, "In the beginning God created the heavens and the earth." Then, as the story unfolds, we see God speaking everything into existence with power and ease. Amazingly, as you read through the creation account, God simply says, "Let there be …" or simply "Let …" and through His word, everything comes into existence. But the process of creation is a bit different when he decides to create mankind. In Genesis 1:26, God says, "Let Us make man in Our image, according to Our likeness."

Wait a second! At that moment, God stops and decides to pour out the entire essence of His being into forming man. A little later in chapter two, verse seven, we get more detail, "then the LORD God formed the man of dust from the ground and breathed into his nostrils the breath of life, and the man became a living creature." The word for breath in Hebrew is *ruach* means "wind," "breath," or "spirit." In essence, God's *ruach* is the source of life. The *ruach* of God is the One who gives life to all creation.

These verses demonstrate God's intimate involvement in creating mankind with his "hands" and in his image, and breathing life into infused His essence into man. To further elaborate on how special we are, God then assigns mankind responsibility and authority to govern his creation under His supervision. Genesis 1:26, He states, "so that they may rule over the fish in the sea and the birds in the sky, over the livestock and all the wild animals, and over all the creatures that move along the ground."

These verses blow my mind because nowhere else does God's creation receive such personal, hands-on attention and assignment of authority. These verses reflect on God's creation of man and how Adam was the crowning achievement of created perfection.

FX3 DAILY DIRECTIVE:

READ:

For you formed my inward parts; you knitted me together in my mother's womb.[14] *I praise you, for I am fearfully and wonderfully made. Wonderful are your works; my soul knows it very well.* - **Psalm 139:13-14**

PRAY:

As you prepare to study, pray for the wisdom to understand and apply what you just read. Journal your prayer.

_____

_____

_____

_____

_____

_____

MEDITATE / MAKE IT REAL:

What does it mean for you to be *fearfully and wonderfully made*?

_____

_____

_____

_____

_____

_____

_____

MEDITATE / MAKE IT REAL:

According to this passage(s), what am I called to do?

_____

_____

_____

_____

_____

_____

How am I going to apply or do what it says?

_____

_____

_____

_____

_____

_____

SHARE:

Share what you've learned with others.

_____

_____

_____

_____

_____

_____

THE SOURCE
THE DISEASE

Shortly after, the Lord God says, "It is not good for the man to be alone. I will make a helper suitable for him." He follows this up by creating all of the living creatures and brings them to Adam. Once again, he tasks him with the honor and responsibility of naming the animals. Yet, none of these serves as a suitable helper for Adam. At that moment, God decides he will take a part of Adam and create his helper.

As a result, God makes the woman and brings her to Adam. Upon seeing this marvelous creation, he is honored and proceeds to name her woman as "she was taken out of man." What ensues is a perfect state of blissful companionship and fellowship with God. Both Adam and the woman "walk" with God. Unfortunately, this state of perfect communion with God and each other is destroyed when the devil shows up on the scene.

There's an interaction with the devil and the woman whereby the devil actively works to dismantle God and Adam's authority all at once. To do this, he has the woman questioning God, and then, in turn, she does the same to Adam. Tragically, Adam goes along with the erroneous belief and shares the fruit with the woman. Adam decides to deliberately disobey God despite knowing the commandments. Consequently, Adam and the woman are guilty of sinning against God. The disease of sin now enters humanity.

First, God passes judgment on everyone and tells them they will now experience death due to their sin. Not only is this a physical, but also a spiritual death transpires. In addition to this, God forewarns them that they will all experience hardship, opposition, and challenges in their lives.

Because of the fall, we're all subject to the disease of sin and illness of the sinful nature. This terrible disease plagues all humanity and is the root of all our problems.

FX3 DAILY DIRECTIVE:

READ:

And to Adam he said, "Because you have listened to the voice of your wife and have eaten of the tree of which I commanded you, 'You shall not eat of it,'cursed is the ground because of you; in pain you shall eat of it all the days of your life; [18] thorns and thistles it shall bring forth for you; and you shall eat the plants of the field. [19] By the sweat of your face you shall eat bread, till you return to the ground, for out of it you were taken; for you are dust, and to dust you shall return." - **Genesis 3:17-19**

PRAY:

As you prepare to study, pray for the wisdom to understand and apply what you just read. Journal your prayer.

_____

_____

_____

_____

_____

_____

MEDITATE / MAKE IT REAL:

How does Adam's decision affect you today?

_____

_____

_____

_____

_____

_____

_____

MEDITATE / MAKE IT REAL: □

According to this passage(s), what am I called to do?

_____

_____

_____

_____

_____

_____

How am I going to apply or do what it says?

_____

_____

_____

_____

_____

_____

SHARE:

Share what you've learned with others.

_____

_____

_____

_____

_____

_____

THE SOURCE
THE ILLNESS

There's a great misconception among Christians today, and that is that when we come to Christ, all of our past issues, hurts, pains, or I say, illnesses immediately disappear. You know the saying, "Time heals all wounds?" Unfortunately, it's not necessarily true. While I have seen addicts break their habits overnight and others transform instantly, most of us continue to struggle with our illnesses. We tend to forget that although we're saved from eternal damnation, our soul is still contained within the sinful flesh. This reality means that our saved soul will continue to wage against the sinful nature of our flesh. When sin entered the world, it brought about the disease of sin and the illness of the sinful nature.

You know that the disease of sin and the result of spiritual death is overcome only through the redemptive blood of Christ. However, this freeing knowledge is only the beginning. The reality, however, is that the Spirit made alive in us still resides in a sinful vessel. This struggle affects us in more ways than we understand. The exact sin nature that plagued the great men of the Bible also plagues us. Left unchecked, we will naturally choose to do what we, or better said, the flesh desires. Charles Spurgeon eloquently once said, "As the salt flavors every drop in the Atlantic, so does sin affect every atom of our nature. It is so sadly there, so abundantly there, that if you cannot detect it, you are deceived." This notion is at the heart of the doctrine of Total Depravity.

Total depravity is a phrase or name used to summarize what the Bible teaches about the spiritual condition of fallen man. The doctrine of total depravity is an acknowledgment that the Bible teaches that as a result of the fall of man (Genesis 3:6), every aspect of man—his mind, will, emotions, and flesh—has been corrupted by sin. However, this does not mean that sin runs rampant in us to the point it overtakes us, and we become pure evil. When all seems lost, Jesus reminds us in Matthew 19:26 that *"With people this is impossible, but with God all things are possible."*

FX3 DAILY DIRECTIVE:

READ:

Formerly, when you did not know God, you were enslaved to those that by nature are not gods. [9] But now that you have come to know God, or rather to be known by God, how can you turn back again to the weak and worthless elementary principles of the world, whose slaves you want to be once more? - **Galatians 4:8-9**

PRAY:

As you prepare to study, pray for the wisdom to understand and apply what you just read. Journal your prayer.

MEDITATE / MAKE IT REAL:

What does it mean for you to be free from the bondage of sin?

MEDITATE / MAKE IT REAL:

According to this passage(s), what am I called to do?

_____

_____

_____

_____

_____

_____

How am I going to apply or do what it says?

_____

_____

_____

_____

_____

_____

SHARE:

Share what you've learned with others.

_____

_____

_____

_____

_____

_____

Jehovah translates as "The Existing One" or "Lord." The meaning of Jehovah comes from the Hebrew word "*havah*" meaning "to be" or "to exist." *Rapha* (râpâ') means "to restore," "to heal," or "to make healthful" in Hebrew. The combination of these two words, Jehovah Rapha, translates to "Jehovah Who Heals." We find this name in various books of the Old Testament. One of the first places we find this name is in Exodus 15:26. In that verse, God says to the people of Israel, "If you listen carefully to the Lord your God and do what is right in his eyes, if you pay attention to his commands and keep all his decrees, I will not bring on you any of the diseases I brought on the Egyptians, for I am the Lord, who heals you."

In the New Testament, we see the incarnation of God through Jesus as the Great Physician in Matthew 9:9-13. Imagine this, Jesus invites a tax collector, despised, and reviled by his people, to "follow" him. It was common knowledge that the publicans or tax collectors cheated their people and had power because they had the backing of the Roman Empire. For the most part, they were "untouchable." This disparity of wealth and power only helped to alienate them from their fellow Jews further. The Pharisees distinctly segmented the worst of the worst into two groups, sinners and tax collectors.

Considering this, imagine when Matthew, a new disciple of Jesus and tax collector himself, decides to put on a dinner for Jesus and invite everyone he knows. This band of deviants includes all his cronies, other tax collectors, and sinners. At that moment, we read how Jesus is comfortably reclining and partaking with these outcasts, and the religious leaders ask why He's associating with these people. Jesus' beautiful response to this criticism? "Those who are well have no need of a physician, but those who are sick. Go and learn what this means: 'I desire mercy, and not sacrifice.' For I came not to call the righteous, but sinners."

FX3 DAILY DIRECTIVE:

READ:

And when the Pharisees saw this, they said to his disciples, "Why does your teacher eat with tax collectors and sinners?" ¹² But when he heard it, he said, "Those who are well have no need of a physician, but those who are sick. ¹³ Go and learn what this means: 'I desire mercy, and not sacrifice.' For I came not to call the righteous, but sinners" -

Matthew 9:11-13

PRAY:

As you prepare to study, pray for the wisdom to understand and apply what you just read. Journal your prayer.

_____

_____

_____

_____

_____

_____

MEDITATE / MAKE IT REAL:

What area(s) in your life need healing?

_____

_____

_____

_____

_____

_____

_____

MEDITATE / MAKE IT REAL: □

According to this passage(s), what am I called to do?

_____

_____

_____

_____

_____

_____

How am I going to apply or do what it says?

_____

_____

_____

_____

_____

_____

SHARE:

Share what you've learned with others.

_____

_____

_____

_____

_____

_____

Before 1967, most heart surgeries focused on correcting congenital heart defects and treating valve disease. However, an ambitious and hopeful Dr. Barnard started to consider the possibilities and potential of open-heart surgery. Finally, after years of intensive study, training, research, experimentation, and experience, Barnard felt he was ready to perform the world's first heart transplant. The opportunity came when Velva ('Val') Schrire, a professor of cardiology, recommended Louis Waskansky, a 53-year-old diabetic bedridden in the hospital with severe cardiac failure from ischemic heart disease, for the operation. Washkansky excitedly accepted the opportunity as he knew this was probably his last hope of staying alive. Then on December 2nd, 1967, Denise Darvall, a 25-year-old woman who suffered a severe brain injury from an accident, was taken to the same hospital. Within hours of being declared brain-dead, her father gave consent to use her heart and kidneys for transplantation.

Shortly after, they took Louis and Denise to the operating room suite, and the operation took place during the early hours of December 3rd. After transplanting the heart, the surgical team waited for the donor heart to beat for what seemed like an eternity but was only a few minutes. After mutiple interventions and stressful situaitons, the beats got stronger, and the blood pressure rose sufficiently enough for him to remove the patient from the heart-lung machine. After five hours, the operation was successful.

Unfortunately, Mr. Washkansky's health deteriorated rapidly shortly after the operation, and he died only 18 days after the transplant. Undeterred by his mission to help others heal, Dr. Barnard continued performing more surgeries and learned more with every subsequent heart transplant. This remarkable story reminds me of how Dr. Barnard helped save lives by replacing a bad and failing heart with a good one yet could not give them a "new" heart. Scripture tells us there is only one physician who can do this, Christ.

FX3 DAILY DIRECTIVE:

READ:

And I will give them one heart, and a new spirit I will put within them. I will remove the heart of stone from their flesh and give them a heart of flesh,
Ezekiel 11:19

PRAY:

As you prepare to study, pray for the wisdom to understand and apply what you just read. Journal your prayer.

_____

_____

_____

_____

_____

_____

MEDITATE / MAKE IT REAL:

What does it mean for God to give you a new heart?

_____

_____

_____

_____

_____

_____

_____

MEDITATE / MAKE IT REAL:

According to this passage(s), what am I called to do?

_____

_____

_____

_____

_____

How am I going to apply or do what it says?

_____

_____

_____

_____

_____

SHARE:

Share what you've learned with others.

_____

_____

_____

_____

_____

FX3 DAILY DIRECTIVE: _____

READ:

PRAY:

As you prepare to study, pray for the wisdom to understand and apply what you just read. Journal your prayer.

_____

_____

_____

_____

_____

_____

_____

MEDITATE / MAKE IT REAL:

How do I see myself in the passage(s) I just read?

_____

_____

_____

_____

_____

_____

_____

_____

MEDITATE / MAKE IT REAL:

According to this passage(s), what am I called to do?

_____

_____

_____

_____

_____

How am I going to apply or do what it says?

_____

_____

_____

_____

_____

SHARE:

Share what you've learned with others.

_____

_____

_____

_____

_____

FX3 DAILY DIRECTIVE: _____

READ:

PRAY:

As you prepare to study, pray for the wisdom to understand and apply what you just read. Journal your prayer.

_____

_____

_____

_____

_____

_____

_____

MEDITATE / MAKE IT REAL:

How do I see myself in the passage(s) I just read?

_____

_____

_____

_____

_____

_____

_____

_____

MEDITATE / MAKE IT REAL:

According to this passage(s), what am I called to do?

_____

_____

_____

_____

_____

_____

How am I going to apply or do what it says?

_____

_____

_____

_____

_____

SHARE:

Share what you've learned with others.

_____

_____

_____

_____

_____

_____

REVIEW & REFLECT

ROMANS 12:2

Do not be conformed to this world, but be transformed by the renewal of your mind, that by testing you may discern what is the will of God, what is good and acceptable and perfect

Not long ago, I was visiting a client's office and was working on some label designs for them. As I clicked away on the computer, a young man greeted me. "You're Marcos, right?" he asked. "Carlos," I replied. "Yes, yes, you've told me that before." He then talked about his job and smoothly interjected that Christ was his Lord and Savior. He then asked me if I was a Christian. "Indeed, brother," I replied. Cesar then started to give me his testimony and excitement of accepting Christ as his Savior a little less than a year ago.

We discussed his commitment, everything he's learning, his amazement of God's grace, and how he wants to share this good news with everyone. Caesar also said that some people told him he's too "fanatical" for the choices he's making to live a holy life for Christ. "Brother, I and many more Christians need that desire you have," I told him. I then encouraged him to continue his passionate pursuit of God and make the spiritual disciplines of reading, praying, and meditating on God's word an everyday priority.

Cesar's story reminds other Christians and me never to forget our first love (Rev 2:4-5). To continually remind ourselves how Christ saved us from eternal death and an unfulfilled life by paying the ultimate price when we didn't, nor deserve. We are a royal priesthood, redeemed, restored, and undergoing a continual process of sanctification by God through the Holy Spirit. May we never lose or take for granted the wonderful gift of salvation and be eternally grateful for his grace. This week you will review and reflect on everything you've learned throughout the past thirty days and next steps.

WHAT WERE SOME KEY TAKEAWAYS FOR YOU DURING THESE 30 DAYS?

WHAT WILL YOU DO WITH EVERYTHING YOU LEARNED? WHERE WILL YOU START?

RECITE OR WRITE THE FOLLOWING VERSES FROM MEMORY:

SESSION 1: PSALM 139:14

_____

_____

_____

SESSION 2: 1 PETER 2:9

_____

_____

_____

SESSION 3: JOHN 8:44

_____

_____

_____

SESSION 4: ROMANS 5:12

_____

_____

_____

REVIEW & REFLECT: ROMANS 12:2

_____

_____

_____

NOTES:

NOTES:

NOTES:

NOTES:

PRAYER REQUESTS:

PRAYER REQUESTS:

_____

_____

_____

_____

_____

_____

_____

_____

_____

_____

_____

_____

_____

_____

_____

_____

_____

_____

_____

_____

_____

_____

_____

_____

_____

PRAYER REQUESTS:

PRAYER REQUESTS:

_____
_____
_____
_____
_____
_____
_____
_____
_____
_____
_____
_____
_____
_____
_____
_____
_____
_____
_____
_____
_____
_____
_____
_____
_____

DAILY DIRECTIVE COMPLETION TRACKER

Below are thirty boxes to help you to track your progress.
After completing a Daily D:
1. Check off the box that corresponds with the day.
2. When you check off seven boxes, celebrate your accomplishment.
3. Remember, be persistent until you are consistent.

DAILY DIRECTIVES - SESSION 1

01	02	03	04	05	06	07

DAILY DIRECTIVES - SESSION 2

08	09	10	11	12	13	14

DAILY DIRECTIVES - SESSION 3

15	16	17	18	19	20	21

DAILY DIRECTIVES - SESSION 4

22	23	24	25	26	27	28

29	30

CONGRATS!

You've just completed Phase 1 of the FX3 Challenge, and I want you to know that you are among a select group of other men on their way to becoming FX3 Warriors. As a Warrior, you're part of a brotherhood that works together to help each other live radically fulfilling and productive lives. The goal, to be the man God desires you to be.

WHAT'S NEXT?

Now that you've completed Phase 1 - FX3 Faith, you're now ready to move unto Phase 2 - FX3 Fire. For more information and resources, visit:
https://faithfirefury.com/fx3-challenge

Made in the USA
Columbia, SC
15 November 2022